Where Is Wisconsin?

Where Is Wisconsin?

by Annette Whipple

illustrated by Ted Hammond

Penguin Workshop

To all readers who celebrate curiosity—AW

PENGUIN WORKSHOP
An imprint of Penguin Random House LLC
1745 Broadway, New York, NY 10019
penguinrandomhouse.com

Designed and Produced by Dinardo Design, LLC.

Library of Congress Cataloging-in-Publication Data is available.

First published in the United States of America by Penguin Workshop, 2026

Manufactured in the United States of America
CJKW

ISBN 9798217244133 (paperback)
10 9 8 7 6 5 4 3 2 1

ISBN 9798217244140 (library binding)
10 9 8 7 6 5 4 3 2 1

The authorized representative in the EU for product safety and compliance is Penguin Random House Ireland, Morrison Chambers, 32 Nassau Street, Dublin D02 YH68, Ireland, https://eu-contact.penguin.ie.

Contents

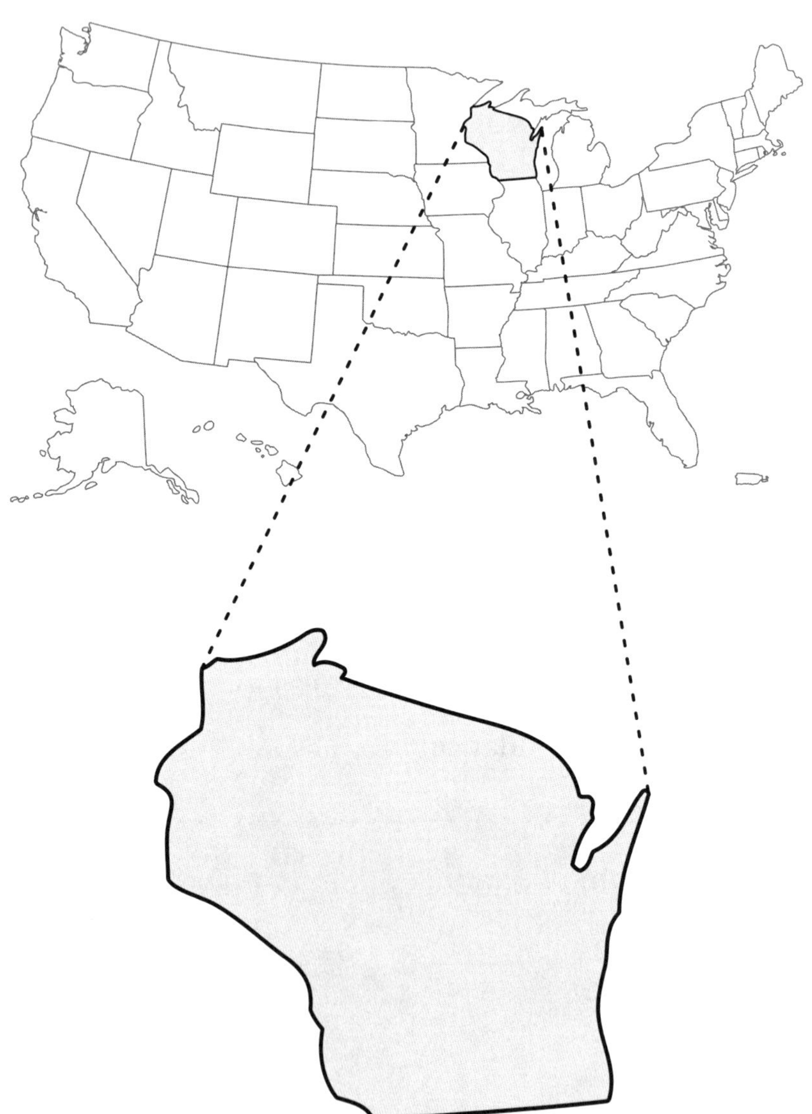

Where Is Wisconsin?

Rival football fans call Green Bay Packers fans cheeseheads. Though intended as an insult, Ralph Bruno embraced the nickname because he liked cheese and was proud that his home state of Wisconsin made so much of it. Cheese making is one of many immigrant traditions the people of Wisconsin celebrate.

Bruno was helping his mom cover her couch with fabric when he had an idea. He cut a couch cushion into a triangle to look like a wedge of cheese. He added holes and painted it yellow. He turned it into a hat. Then he wore the cheesehead hat to a sporting event. It attracted so much attention that his friends wanted to be cheeseheads, too. He started a trend!

Cheesehead hats became famous. Packers fans

wear the hats to the team's National Football League (NFL) games. Today, people from Wisconsin are proud to be called cheeseheads—even if they don't wear a cheese-shaped hat!

CHAPTER 1
Wisconsin and First People

Wisconsin is famous for its cheese, but it has lots more to offer. It covers nearly fifty-five thousand square miles and includes a variety of natural features. Located in the Midwest, Wisconsin borders the Mississippi River and two Great Lakes. Along the northern border, Lake Superior's shoreline stretches for 150 miles. It is the biggest, deepest, and coldest of the Great Lakes. The eastern border of Wisconsin is formed by Lake Michigan.

The state also has more than sixteen thousand lakes and eighty-four thousand miles of rivers and streams. The Apostle Islands National Lakeshore includes old-growth forests, sea caves, and sandy beaches on twenty-one islands along Lake

Superior. More than five miles of the Wisconsin River feature towering cliffs, canyons, and rock formations called the Dells of the Wisconsin River. The formations are created by wind and water wearing away at the rock surface through a process called erosion. In the north, forests cover nearly one-third of the state. Few trees grow in the southern prairies (open grasslands). The east has lowlands and gentle hills, with soil that is good for farming. Valleys cover much of the west.

The weather in Wisconsin affects how people work and play every day. Though it has four distinct seasons, Wisconsin's winters are long and cold. Some parts of the state average more than 150 inches of snow every year. Spring thaws lead to short, warm summers. Colorful leaves brighten the landscape during the fall.

The forests, prairies, and lakes provide diverse habitats and homes for a wide variety of plants and animals. Black bears, moose, and legless glass lizards make their homes in Wisconsin. The world's fastest bird lives in Wisconsin, too. Though able to fly at speeds of 240 miles per hour, peregrine (say: PEH-ruh-grin) falcons have needed protection for more than fifty years because they are at risk of extinction (dying out). About forty nesting boxes have been put on Wisconsin's tall buildings for the birds. Every year since 1998, a pair of peregrine falcons returns to a Manitowoc (say: MAN-i-tuh-wok) nesting box at the top of a grain elevator. The efforts have helped increase the population of peregrine falcons.

Long ago, this area was home to a huge mammal: woolly mammoths! One of the largest and most complete woolly mammoth skeletons ever excavated (dug out of the earth) was found in Wisconsin. The bones are about 14,500 years old and have markings that show people lived in the region at that time.

Some of the early people who made their

homes in what we now call Wisconsin were Paleo-Indians. They hunted large animals, such as woolly mammoths, mastodons, and bison. As early as 700 BCE, the Woodland culture arrived. They were some of the first to grow corn, make pottery, and use the bow and arrow. Eventually, they built effigy mounds (large burial hills). Some were shaped like birds, deer, bears, or other animals.

A rabbit-shaped effigy mound in Madison, Wisconsin

A group of people from the Mississippian culture migrated to the area around 1000 CE. They built towns and traded pottery. The Mississippians left the area after two hundred years, but the Oneota soon arrived. The Dakota (also called Sioux), Ho-Chunk (also called Winnebago), and Menominee (say: muh-NAA-muh-nee) Nations are likely descendants of the Oneota.

More nations migrated to the land around 1500, including the Sauk, Potawatomi (say: POT-uh-wat-oh-mee), and Ottawa. With so many groups, there were many unique languages, customs, and beliefs in the land we call Wisconsin.

Things began to change for the Indigenous nations when Europeans arrived. In 1634, a French explorer named Jean Nicolet came to the shores of what is now Green Bay. He had been hired by the governor of New France (now called Canada). He knew some Indigenous languages and was sent there to make peace with the Indigenous peoples and explore the land. He met with representatives of the Ho-Chunk Nation before French traders arrived. More European settlers followed.

When European explorers came to the area, they wrote about a river. Though its name has been spelled many different ways, some historians think the word *Wisconsin* is a European version of what the Miami Nation called the Wisconsin River. Their name for it meant "river running through a red place." Reddish cliff rocks and stone in the Wisconsin Dells likely inspired it. Soon, the area near the river became known as Wisconsin.

Some fur traders arrived in Wisconsin starting around 1655. Most were from France. They built homes and set up trading posts. Indigenous hunters and trappers brought beaver pelts and other furs to trade. Trading posts were a type of store and became more common in Wisconsin in the late 1600s and early 1700s. The posts had goods, such as metal tools, knives, cooking kettles, steel flints to start fires, guns, and ammunition. They also had wool blankets, alcohol, and glass beads.

The owners of trading posts didn't want money. Animal pelts were worth far more. Beaver skins were especially valuable because they were turned into warm, waterproof hats. Instead of paying with money, many Indigenous people traded fur pelts for store goods. Later, the traders packed up big canoes with thousands of pelts and made yearly trips to Montreal. The pelts were sold in New France as well as in Europe. The Wisconsin and Fox Rivers were important for shipping goods.

With news of the good hunting in the area, more Europeans settled nearby, including many British people. Conflicts arose between the French, British, and Indigenous trappers because the animal furs were so profitable. Outside of Wisconsin, Britain and France fought the French and Indian War between 1754 and 1763. The French had the help of some Indigenous people, but the British won the war. Since the French lost, Britain now controlled the fur trade.

European settlers brought diseases new to the area, such as smallpox. They were dangerous to Indigenous communities. As many as 90 percent of the Indigenous people in the area died. In the East, settlers took over the land and drove Indigenous nations away. Many moved to Wisconsin. More settlers arrived, too. Some newcomers farmed and grew wheat and other crops, but many also hunted and trapped.

This led to further competition for land and hunting rights. Many white settlers felt they had a right to the Wisconsin land that Indigenous people had lived on for thousands of years. Some settlers took land by force. In 1712, French settlers killed nearly 1,500 Meskwaki (say: mess-KWACK-ee), also called Fox, and Mascouten (say: mas-COO-ten) people.

In addition to the violence and disease, Indigenous cultures and ways of life changed dramatically because of the trading posts set up by European traders. Previously, Indigenous people had used tools they could make, including clay pots, stone tools, and bows and arrows. In time, those items were replaced with brass kettles, iron axes, and guns. Those goods became necessary, but people needed the trading posts to get the items. By 1760, some Indigenous communities went from mostly farming with seasonal hunting to full-time hunting and trapping.

As more people came to the area, a war was being fought to the east. In 1776, thirteen British colonies along the East Coast rebelled and declared their independence. The war called the American Revolution ended in 1783. The British had to give the land of Wisconsin to the newly formed United States of America.

CHAPTER 2
Early Wisconsin

After the United States won its independence, even more settlers came to Wisconsin. Some farmed. Others wanted to work as miners.

Indigenous people had been mining the mineral of lead (say: LED) ore for over a hundred years by the early 1800s. That's when European settlers also began to mine in the area. Lead was useful to make paint, ammunition, and pewter (a strong metal). In 1828, Willis St. John bought a cave from Indigenous people. St. John expanded mining operations to collect more lead from the cave. This mine and others in southern Wisconsin attracted more miners and further displaced Indigenous communities.

At first, many new miners didn't take the time

to build homes. They dug shelters in the ground known as badger holes—like the animals' homes. Eventually, Wisconsin even became nicknamed the Badger State. The nickname didn't come from the animal but from the miners who lived in those simple holes.

Over time, homes were built near the mines in the area and communities grew. Towns developed as other businesses were set up. Mining became very profitable, with thirteen million pounds of lead ore removed from the ground in 1829.

Immigrants from Cornwall, England, settled primarily in an area called Mineral Point. Their mining experience from before they'd come to the United States helped them to dig deeper when the surface lead ran out. By 1829, the town mined millions of pounds of lead every year. Eventually, some of the workers left to mine iron, zinc, or copper in other locations. Some went as far as California during the gold rush of 1849. Others learned that the mining region they'd moved to was also great for farming.

Farming for profit (and not just one family's needs) grew in popularity. Some people milked cows on dairy farms. These Wisconsin farmers knew cheese lasted longer than milk or butter before going bad. Charles Rockwell began making cheese in Koshkonong (say: KOASH-koh-nong) as early as 1837. Just four years later, Anne Pickett used her neighbor's milk in her cheese factory. J. I. Smith didn't make cheese just for his community. He shipped barrels of cheese to Chicago. By the 1840s, Wisconsin had many successful cheese makers with a wide variety of flavors.

In addition to dairy farms, crops, including wheat, oats, and cranberries, became popular. Barley was especially common. Many towns had their own breweries and used barley grain to make beer. The city of Milwaukee had multiple breweries.

The lumber industry also grew in the 1800s. Lumberjacks cut trees in the forests along the Wisconsin River. The logs floated downstream to sawmills, where they became usable lumber such as boards. Stores, banks, and other businesses near sawmills became towns and cities.

European communities grew as settlers came to the area. Additional Indigenous groups also arrived. They had been forced to leave their homes in the East. Electa Quinney was a Mohican woman

and teacher from New York. She saw the need for a public school in Wisconsin. Quinney began the first public school in Wisconsin in 1828. It was in Kakauna (say: KAH-kahn-uh), along the Fox River. She taught white and Indigenous children.

The population in the area continued to increase. The land was officially named Wisconsin Territory in 1836. Madison was chosen as its capital, where government decisions would be made.

Wisconsin Territory didn't allow slavery, but it was legal in other parts of the United States. With the territory between the country's northern border of Canada (where slavery wasn't allowed) and Missouri (a nearby state where slavery was legal), some people in Wisconsin became part of the Underground Railroad. It wasn't underground, and it wasn't a railroad. Instead, it was a secret network of people and places that helped freedom seekers escape to Canada.

The first known freedom seeker to come through Wisconsin was a sixteen-year-old named Caroline Quarlls. She escaped slavery in St. Louis, Missouri, in 1842. After she made it to Wisconsin, abolitionists who wanted to stop slavery helped her get to Canada safely.

With a population of about three hundred thousand, Wisconsin became the thirtieth state on May 29, 1848. By 1850, Wisconsin had more than a thousand schools. Most schools were for students between first and eighth grade. The very first kindergarten in the United States was founded by a German immigrant in Watertown. The state already had a few colleges, including its first, Carroll College (now called Carroll University).

The Republican Party was founded in Wisconsin in 1854, with a major goal of opposing slavery. It gained support across the state and nation. In 1860, Abraham Lincoln became the first Republican to be elected as president of the United States. With a Republican as president, the Southern states expected that Lincoln would abolish slavery, making it illegal. So, the United States divided, and the Civil War began in 1861. The Union (Northern states) supported ending slavery, and the Confederacy (Southern states) wanted slavery to continue.

Most of the people of Wisconsin supported the Union. Many volunteered as soldiers. The state sent more than ninety-one thousand soldiers to the Civil War, including more than three hundred Black men.

Wisconsin soldiers served in all of the major battles in states, including Virginia, Maryland, and Pennsylvania. More than twelve thousand Wisconsin men died fighting in the Civil War by the time it ended in 1865.

The Republican Party

When some Wisconsinites began to discuss allowing slavery in the state, a lot of people disapproved. Many immigrants (who made up most of the population) generally opposed slavery. Newspaper writers shared their opinions against slavery, too. Some politicians who made laws met in Ripon to talk about how they could stop slavery from being legalized in the state.

The meeting included people from various political parties. They had very different ideas about leading the government. Stopping slavery was so important that these members of the Whig, Free Soil, and Democratic parties came together. They united as a new political party that would oppose slavery. They became the Republican Party in 1854.

After the Civil War, Milwaukee continued to be an important manufacturing center. Allis Company made machines and equipment for flour mills, farms, and mines. Papermaking became big along the Fox River. Shipbuilding expanded along Lake Superior, Lake Michigan, and Sturgeon Bay. Wisconsin was still a leader in barley production, too, and Milwaukee was

important in the brewing industry.

When wheat crops failed, dairy farms became more common. Many dairy farmers had experience from New York, where they'd moved from. Their skills, combined with research from the University of Wisconsin, helped dairy farmers become very successful in the state. There was such a demand for Wisconsin cheese that fifty-four factories made cheese there by 1870. Wisconsin's immigrants had brought their traditional cheese making to the state. They produced cheeses such as Gouda (Dutch), Swiss (Swiss), cheddar (British), Brie (French), mozzarella (Italian), and Muenster (German). They also created new flavors, such as Brick and Colby. Wisconsin became famous for its cheese.

Wisconsin was a state of many firsts, including a milk-testing invention that measured butterfat in milk. High amounts of butterfat made the best cheese. The typewriter, automobile, and malted milk were also invented there. The town of Two Rivers claims they served the first ice-cream sundae!

The state held the first Ringling Brothers performance. Five brothers put on a backyard show with dancing and singing. They used the profits from the show to buy suits and top hats and then took their show on the road. Eventually, it became a traveling circus, famously called the Greatest Show on Earth. Wisconsin was an industrial and business powerhouse, and it was just getting started.

CHAPTER 3
The Making of Modern Wisconsin

With big companies in Wisconsin, there was a need for trade schools (also called technical colleges). They trained teens and adults for work at these companies, as well as other industries. Although most of these schools were for men, two Milwaukee public high schools had programs for women.

Wisconsin continued to draw immigrants from around the world, and a variety of work was available. Many people found employment in factories. Others worked in mines or in the lumber industry. Some had farms or small businesses. Additional work opportunities included railroads, cranberry harvesting, meatpacking plants, and tanneries (which make leather). Though

Wisconsin companies employed many people, Black people experienced prejudice. They could do the work just as well but often wouldn't be hired.

World War I began in 1914 and lasted four years. The fighting mostly took place in Europe and the Middle East. About 118,000 soldiers from Wisconsin served in the war.

America fought against a group of countries that included Germany. In the United States, many people became scared of Germans and wanted to remove all traces of Germany from their lives. They even changed the names of things. Wieners became hot dogs.

People burned German books and banned the use of German language in schools. Towns and buildings were renamed. Orchestras stopped performing songs composed by Bach (say: BOCK) and Beethoven (say: bay-TOE-vin), who were both German. There was even a fear that some German Americans might be spies. Many were accused without reason. It was a dangerous time for German Americans. People formerly proud of their German heritage became frightened. Many changed their names so their German roots would be hidden.

This happened throughout the country and especially in Milwaukee. The hatred for things related to Germany was particularly hard because of the immigrant population of Wisconsin. In the early 1900s, German Americans were the largest ethnic group in the state. They made up nearly half of all the foreign-born people in Wisconsin.

Tensions eased after the war ended. In 1919, Wisconsin was the first state to ratify, or approve, the Nineteenth Amendment to the Constitution and give American women the right to vote. Women accomplished important things in the state. In Milwaukee, Lizzie Black Kander and other Jewish women started an organization that

gave classes on history and cooking. They offered athletic and cultural clubs. During the Great Depression, which began in 1929, Kander started one of the country's first food exchanges. People could get food at a very low cost.

The Great Depression was a time when there was little money, even for food. Many businesses and factories couldn't pay their employees. People lost their jobs. To help Americans, city, state, and national programs provided jobs. Programs like Kander's food exchange helped, too. By helping one another, people in Wisconsin built a stronger sense of community.

The people of Wisconsin unified—including when the United States entered World War II in 1941. They volunteered as soldiers and nurses. More than three hundred thousand people from Wisconsin served in the military all over the world. Milwaukee made important weapons and machines for the war effort. When the war ended in 1945, Wisconsinites celebrated together.

In 1964, the nation passed the Civil Rights Act. This law ended segregation, which had kept white and Black people separate in public spaces. Supporters, led by Black Americans, worked for equality and an end to all racist laws and attitudes in Wisconsin, too. It took many years, but finally Black people in Wisconsin had access to better schooling, work, and housing. It wasn't until 1976 that Milwaukee's public schools were officially ordered to desegregate by a judge.

The civil rights movement also helped Latino and Indigenous people push for equal rights and fair treatment. They fought against discrimination and called for public schools to teach lessons in multiple languages so their children could learn more easily.

Television viewers across America tuned in to watch a Milwaukee family in the show called *Happy Days* from 1974 to 1984. This popular show led to more Milwaukee-set shows, such as *Laverne and Shirley*, which was about two roommates who worked in a Milwaukee brewery.

On television, viewers also learned about state news. In 1980, a terrible windstorm struck

Wisconsin during a heat wave. Damaging winds hit at 110 miles per hour. They broke an anemometer, which measures wind speed! The storm devastated about 4,800 square miles. It caused 160 million dollars in damage! (That would be nearly a billion dollars today.) It was the worst storm the state had ever experienced, with destroyed buildings, downed trees, and blocked roads. But neighbors helped neighbors—and strangers. Without electricity, meat thawed in freezers but couldn't be cooked on stoves. Across the city of Eau Claire (say: oh-CLARE), people grilled and shared food, creating a sense of community. Chainsaws cut up trees, and powerlines were restored.

Extreme weather continued to affect Wisconsin. One winter, twenty-three feet of snow fell in the town of Hurley! During a different year, a blizzard created snow drifts as tall as twenty feet. Severe weather during the summers can include

droughts (say: DROWTS) with little rain, as well as high winds. On a June night in southern Wisconsin in 1984, three tornadoes touched down. One destroyed nearly all of the buildings of Barneveld. That tornado was classified as an F5 tornado—the most intense on the rating scale.

Wisconsin's passion for cheese continued. In 1988, cheese makers at Simon's Specialty Cheese created a forty-thousand-pound block of cheddar!

It held the world record for the largest block of cheese for years.

Wisconsin fans began wearing cheesehead hats to events in the late 1980s. Ralph Bruno created the first cheesehead and eventually started a business for these hats, especially for Green Bay Packers football fans. They proudly wore their cheeseheads when the Green Bay Packers won the Super Bowl in 1997 and again in 2011.

CHAPTER 4
Wisconsin Today

Today, industry continues to be important throughout the state. Tools, farm equipment, and engines are made in Milwaukee. Meat-packers prepare meat for shipment to stores. Forest products, such as lumber, contribute to Wisconsin's economy. Harley-Davidson motorcycles have been made in Wisconsin for over a hundred years.

The city of Green Bay, along the Fox River, is home to mills that manufacture paper. A company in Racine makes Case IH tractors. Oshkosh became famous for children's clothing with the brand OshKosh B'Gosh. Miller beer, Trek bikes, and American Girl all began in Wisconsin. There's another famous doll who is from Wisconsin: Barbie! She and Ken, though they are made by a California company, are from the fictional town of Willows, Wisconsin.

The Port of Duluth-Superior (on the border of Minnesota and Wisconsin) is the continent's farthest inland freshwater seaport. It's busy with ships docked to load and unload. The port supports many local industries, including health care, transportation, aviation, aerospace, and more. As the Great Lakes cargo capital, over a million tons of grain and twenty million tons of iron ore ship out each season!

Agriculture thrives in Wisconsin. It's the top-ranking state for cranberry production. Potatoes, snap beans, and green peas are also popular. Wisconsin is known as America's Dairyland for a reason: The state has more than five thousand dairy farms—more than any other state!

Over a million cows in Wisconsin produce the milk that has made the state famous for cheese. Wisconsin cheese makers won more awards than any other state or country at the 2024 World Championship Cheese Contest with 117 awards. That same year, they made more than three billion pounds of cheese in more than six hundred different styles!

Tourism is also popular in the state. About 114 million tourists visited Wisconsin in 2024. Lake Minocqua (say: min-AH-kwa) is a year-round favorite with skiing, snowmobiling, and ice fishing in the winter and water sports, swimming, and fishing the rest of the year. Schoolhouse Beach on Washington Island doesn't have sand. Instead, it has smooth limestone pebbles! Door County is also a top Wisconsin vacation destination. It offers historic lighthouses, small towns, beaches, vineyards, art galleries, theaters, and live performances. Wisconsin Dells is called the Waterpark Capital of the World.

Outdoor recreation is so popular that Wisconsin has fifty state parks, fifteen state forests, and more than forty state trails. Swimming, water sports, and boating are popular activities at the state parks.

Winter sports also bring people together in the state. About fifty teams speed across the snow for the Apostle Islands Sled Dog Race. Spectators gather to watch adults play pond hockey, and snowmobile contestants compete in world championships hosted in Wisconsin.

Summers bring people together with fairs. About forty thousand people attend the Wisconsin State Cow Chip Throw & Festival, where the record for throwing dried cow dung is 248 feet! More than a million people come together for the Wisconsin State Fair, which was first held in 1851. The fair lasts for eleven days and celebrates the state's agriculture and other industries with exhibits, rides, entertainment, and lots of food!

A lot of Wisconsin's favorite foods celebrate

the diverse cultures of the state. Bratwursts are a German-style sausage. Butter-fried potatoes pressed into a "pancake" and often topped with an egg, bacon, and cheese make the Swiss dish called Rösti (say: RAH-stee). The fruit-filled, flaky Danish pastry called the kringle is the state pastry! Cornish pasties were made by miners' wives in the 1800s as handheld pies and they are still popular. Friday nights combine Catholic, German, and Polish traditions with fish fries. Traditional Indigenous foods such as wild rice and bison meat are still eaten all over the state.

Along with great food, the people of Wisconsin have been passionate about sports for a long time. Baseball fans are loyal to the Milwaukee Brewers of Major League Baseball. Football fans still wear cheesehead hats to cheer on the Green Bay Packers. They've won more championships than any other NFL team in history. Basketball fans went wild when the Milwaukee Bucks won the

National Basketball Association Championship in 2021.

Today, the Indigenous population of the state is over 106,000. The Ho-Chunk Nation is one of eleven federally recognized Indigenous nations in the state. In 2021, a 1,200-year-old dugout canoe was found in Lake Mendota. A group of Ho-Chunk people spent months burning and scraping a log to form a canoe as their ancestors would have. In 2022, they paddled to the site of the ancient canoe. An even older canoe, from three thousand years ago, was found later that year! The canoes may have belonged to Ho-Chunk people based on where they were found.

Nearly six million people make their homes in Wisconsin. Timber, mining, and agriculture continue to be important to the state and the country. Millions of tourists visit the cities, small towns, and lakes for adventure and entertainment. Wisconsin's cheeses feed the world!

Wisconsin at a Glance

Statehood: 1848

Nickname: The Badger State

Abbreviation: WI

State Motto: Forward

State Tree: Sugar maple

State Animal: Badger

Capital: Madison

Size: 65,496 square miles

Population: About 6 million

Famous People from Wisconsin:

Danica Patrick (NASCAR driver), Colin Kaepernick (NFL player and activist), Tony Shalhoub (actor), Laura Ingalls Wilder (author), Frank Lloyd Wright (architect)

State flag

State bird
American robin

State flower
Wood violet

FUN FACT:

Wisconsin has more than sixteen thousand lakes. About half of them cover more than five acres of land each!

Timeline of Wisconsin

1000	Mississippian people migrate to the area
1634	Explorer Jean Nicolet arrives at Green Bay shores
1828	Willis St. John buys a lead mine
	Electa Quinney founds the first public school in Wisconsin
1837	Charles Rockwell begins making cheese
1848	Wisconsin becomes a state with Madison as its capital
1854	The Republican Party is founded
1856	The first kindergarten in the nation opens
1919	Wisconsin is the first state to approve the Nineteenth Amendment, giving women the right to vote
1974	*Happy Days* debuts on television
1997	The snowiest winter on record in Hurley ends, with 278 inches of total snowfall
2011	The Green Bay Packers win the Super Bowl
2024	Wisconsin cheese makers win the most awards at the 2024 World Championship Cheese Contest

Timeline of the World

1000 — Norse explorer Leif Erikson reaches North America

1607 — Jamestown is founded in the colony of Virginia

1643 — Louis XIV becomes king of France

1703 — Russian ruler Peter the Great founds the city of Saint Petersburg

1760 — The Great Fire of Boston destroys 349 buildings and several ships

1803 — The Great Fire of 1803 burns in Bombay, India

1876 — Alexander Graham Bell makes the first phone call

1914 — The completed Panama Canal connects the Atlantic and Pacific Oceans

1928 — Mickey Mouse appears in Hollywood for the first time

1969 — Neil Armstrong is the first person to walk on the moon

1992 — The World Wide Web becomes available to the public

2020 — The spread of COVID-19 becomes a global pandemic

2024 — About fifteen thousand athletes compete in the Summer Olympics and Paralympics hosted in Paris, France

Bibliography

*Books for young readers

*Franchino, Vicky. ***Wisconsin***. A True Book: My United States. New York: Scholastic Inc., 2018.

*Labrecque, Ellen. ***Who Was Frank Lloyd Wright?*** New York: Penguin Workshop, 2015.

*Wargin, Kathy-jo. ***B is for Badger: A Wisconsin Alphabet***. Ann Arbor, MI: Sleeping Bear Press, 2004.

Websites

Wisconsin Department of Natural Resources: dnr.wisconsin.gov

Wisconsin First Nations: wisconsinfirstnations.org

Wisconsin Historical Society: wisconsinhistory.org

Wisconsin Life: wisconsinlife.org